THE PERFECT MIRROR

THE
PERFECT
MIRROR

edited by

Kenneth D. Macleod

FREE PRESBYTERIAN PUBLICATIONS

FREE PRESBYTERIAN PUBLICATIONS
133 Woodlands Road
Glasgow
G3 6LE

Most of the pieces in this book were previously published in
The Young People's Magazine

This collection first published 1992

ISBN 0 902506 31 5

Origination by
Settle Graphics
Settle, North Yorkshire

Printed by
The Craven Herald & Pioneer
Skipton, North Yorkshire

Contents

Found Out

THIS story is about two American boys, Carl and Benny. They were great friends, but sometimes they got into trouble.

One day they went to Mr. Brown, the shoe repairer, to get new rubber heels put on Carl's shoes. On the way home Benny told Carl, "When I was waiting for you I saw a peach tree behind the shop. It has ripe peaches on it. Let's get some tonight."

"That wouldn't be right," Carl told Benny. "That would be stealing, wouldn't it?" But his mouth watered.

"Oh, we won't take many," answered Benny, "just enough for the two of us. Nobody will ever miss them."

"But what if we get caught," Carl said, looking worried.

But to the peach tree they went that night. Quickly they gathered peaches; then they crept back through the grass. They ran to the barn at Carl's place and hid the peaches there, planning to eat them in the next few days.

In the barn Carl was feeling uneasy. He was pretty sure no one had seen them, but that did not make him feel better.

"Benny, we are thieves!" he suddenly said.

"But nobody saw us," Benny replied.

"Doesn't matter," said Carl. "Just because no one else knows doesn't make any difference. We're still thieves.

The two boys argued for some time until Benny asked, "What are you going to do about it?"

"I'm taking back my share tomorrow," answered Carl. "I don't want to have this awful feeling all the time. I'll just have to tell Mr. Brown that I took them."

Next morning Carl put half the peaches in a bag and went back to Mr. Brown's shop.

"Hello, young man," Mr. Brown said cheerfully. "What can I do for you today?"

"I, um . . . I have some peaches here. . . ."

"Well, well," Mr. Brown said, "so you brought back the peaches you took last night. Where's Benny and his peaches?"

Carl's mouth opened in surprise. "Who told you?"

"Something that can't talk," Mr. Brown said. "Come! I'll show you." Under the peach tree Mr. Brown kneeled down and pointed to some footprints in the soft ground. "You know those new heels I put on your shoes yesterday? I put the very same kind on Benny's shoes last week. They were the only two pairs of that kind that I had left. As soon as I saw these footprints this morning, I knew them. I also saw that some peaches were gone, and I knew who took them. I'm glad you brought them back. Find Benny and bring him here. I have something to say to both of you."

8

Carl found Benny, and they went to Mr. Brown together.

"Boys, I could have reported you to the Police or to your parents, but I decided not to. Instead, I want to talk to you about what really made you take my peaches."

Mr. Brown, who loved the Lord Jesus, explained that every person is born a sinner, and that we all sin. So we need Jesus Christ to save us. Only He can save us from the punishment we deserve for our sins. Mr. Brown explained that they must come to God to tell Him about their sins. He also told them that they had to trust in Jesus Christ, who suffered the punishment for His people's sins by dying on the cross.

Boys and girls, have you ever felt uneasy about your sins, as Carl did about his stealing? Have you realised that "your sin will find you out"? You cannot do wrong and get away with it, as Benny thought. God sees everything we do, and He will punish us for our sins if we are not saved, for "whatsoever a man soweth, that shall he also reap".

Should you not go to God in prayer and tell him about your sins? Yes, indeed; and you should go right away. Ask God to have mercy on you, and to make you willing and able to trust in Jesus Christ to save you from your sins.

The Lord's
My Shepherd

THE Lord's my Shepherd, I'll not want.
He makes me down to lie
In pastures green: He leadeth me
The quiet waters by.

My soul He doth restore again;
And me to walk doth make
Within the paths of righteousness,
Ev'n for His own name's sake.

Yea, though I walk in death's dark vale,
Yet will I fear none ill:
For Thou art with me; and Thy rod
And staff me comfort still.

My table Thou hast furnished
In presence of my foes;
My head Thou dost with oil anoint,
And my cup overflows.

Goodness and mercy all my life
Shall surely follow me:
And in God's house for evermore
My dwelling-place shall be.

Psalm 23

The Perfect
Mirror

THERE was once a very ugly African princess who had always been flattered by her subjects that she was beautiful. But one day a trader came that way and presented her with a mirror. When the princess looked at it and saw how frightfully ugly she was, she became so angry with the mirror that she smashed it to pieces. Fancy being angry with a mirror! It was not the mirror that made her ugly; it only showed her how ugly she really was.

Now the Word of God is very much like that mirror: it shows boys and girls their true likeness, and it is not a flattering picture. It gives a picture of a sinner's heart and shows how ugly it is: ''Deceitful above all things, and desperately wicked.'' The Bible also says, ''There is no difference, for all have sinned''.

People do not like to be told this, and sometimes become very angry at the message, and with the messenger too. One young woman said she would not go back to church because the services made her feel very uncomfortable. She had seen her real picture as a poor lost sinner, and she did not like it. Now surely if someone has a serious disease, it is far better for him to know his real state than to think there is not much the matter with him. If he knows the truth, he may seek and find a cure.

See then that you listen to God when He tells you that you are a sinner, because everything that He says is true. But He also tells you in the Bible that Christ is able to heal you, to cleanse your soul and save you. So He is the Great Physician of souls — a Doctor for our souls, whose cure never fails. Always remember how much *you* need Him to heal your soul, and ask Him to do that for you.

Elephants

ON our recent visit to the Victoria Falls we actually stood on the road while a herd of elephants passed right beside us. While rather alarming, it was also fascinating to see these extraordinary animals at such close quarters — the huge males, the smaller mothers and two or three tinies, already exact replicas of their parents.

They say that elephants never forget. It seems that particular herds come each day to drink from the same place at the river, just near where we were staying. They certainly did not forget this good source of water.

However wonderful these creatures are, we ourselves have been created by the same Creator in a much more wonderful way. We have been made in God's image; we have a living soul. We too, have been given a memory, but how easily we forget! Perhaps you have made up your mind many times to be obedient and helpful at home; perhaps even to seek Christ. Yet how easily and quickly your intention was forgotten! Why is this? It is because we are sinful, and sin affects even our memories!

We need to pray to God to help us to remember what we should remember — especially that we would remember our Creator, God Himself. God says to you,

"Remember now thy Creator in the days of thy youth". You should pray for a new heart so that you would not forget God, for it is wicked to be forgetting Him. You should also ask Him for grace so that you would remember His Word and obey it. David said:

> "And, by Thy grace, I never will
> Thy holy Word forget."

M. Graham

The Huge
Catch of Fish

MOST of Jesus' disciples were fishermen; not the sort of fishermen that go with a rod to the river, but the sort that go out in boats with nets to catch fish. The disciples had been out fishing all night on the lake, but they had caught nothing.

In the morning, when they came ashore, they were washing their nets. Jesus was there and He began to teach the people who crowded round Him on the shore. For safety's sake and so that the people could better see and hear Him, He went into a boat of His disciple, Simon Peter. Simon pushed the boat out a little distance from the shore.

You can imagine how tired the disciples would be by this time, having worked hard all night. So when Jesus' talk was over, they probably expected to get some rest; but no — Jesus told them to push their boats out further and to go fishing!

The disciples would no doubt have been very surprised at this; so Simon Peter, who often did the talking, said, "Master, we have toiled all night and have caught nothing". He seemed to think that there was no point in going fishing, but, being a good man who loved Jesus, he said that they would do so.

So Simon Peter's boat and another boat went fishing; and what do you think happened? They caught lots and lots of fish! In fact, so many, that their net began to break. What excitement there was! They signalled to the other boat to come and help them, and between them they filled both boats so full that they began to sink.

Now, how do you think Simon Peter felt? He had thought, you will remember, that there was no point in going fishing. Well, he would now be embarrassed and ashamed. So what did he do? He went to Jesus to apologise for his bad thoughts and his unbelief. "I am a sinful man," he said to Jesus. He felt so bad about it that he seems to have felt not worthy of being one of Jesus' disciples. "Depart from me; for I am a sinful man, O Lord," he said.

What do you think Jesus said to him? He told him not to be afraid, and that from then on he was to catch men. Why do you think that Jesus said that to Simon Peter? Because Simon Peter had to learn the lesson, at that time, that he was not to doubt Jesus' Word. If he was to preach about Jesus, and catch people so that they would believe in and follow Jesus, then he would need to learn this lesson.

Now, we also can learn a few lessons from this story.

First, we can learn that *we should always believe Jesus,* because He knows better than we can know. Jesus is the Son of God, and therefore He knew that there were fish in the water at that particular place, although Simon Peter did not think so.

Second, even when we do not fully understand, or have some doubts about, what Jesus tells us to do, *we should obey,* as Simon Peter did. He did this out of love to Jesus; and Jesus then took away his doubts and strengthened his faith.

A third lesson is that, when we see that we have done wrong and have sinned against God, *we should confess our sin to Him,* as Simon Peter did. We should also apologise to anyone to whom we have done wrong. It may be that in our doing so, Jesus will make use of us in His work.

There is another lesson that we can learn. Simon Peter was a good fisherman; he had probably learned to fish as a small boy with his father. When he had finished fishing that night, it is likely that he thought that there were no fish to be caught at that time and place. But he was wrong. There were fish. We know that from this story. But it was only when Jesus was with them that they caught the fish. Surely we can learn from this that, no matter how good at any work we may think we are, *we should ask Jesus' help with it.* Boys and girls, when you get up each morning you should remember to go on your knees and ask Jesus to be with you to help you that day, even with those things that you think you know best.

D. M. Boyd

Cathy Kennedy

CATHY KENNEDY was a good girl. She lived in Dingwall, where her father was a minister. When she was just three a lot of children became ill at the same time. Cathy also fell sick. After a while she got better, but she was never really well again.

When I say that Cathy was a good girl, what do I mean? Not, of course, that she never did anything wrong. But there was in her, just as there was in a little boy in Israel in Bible times, "some good thing toward the Lord God". And it was God Himself who put that "good thing" in her, because like everyone else — including you and me — she was, as David put it, "born in sin".

Do you remember how Jesus told Nicodemus that he must be born again? If he was not born again he would not have gone to heaven when he died. Well, Cathy was born again, and it was only God who could have done that for her.

How did people know that Cathy was born again? It was because she was different from children who are not born again. Especially because of the things she liked. For instance, she was often asking her mother to pray with her. And she wanted the Sabbath Day to be kept holy; she was very surprised to find one Sabbath that one of her toys had not been put away the night before.

But the thing that showed more than anything else what God had done for her was how she loved the Bible. Even when she was just two and a half she knew a lot about what the Bible teaches, and while she was sick she learned a lot more.

One day Cathy's back was sore and she asked her mother to rub it. Her mother answered, "I don't like doing it; the bones are so bare".

"But, mother, God could put flesh on my bones; and more than that, He can wash me in His own blood."

"Quite true, dear Cathy, but do you think He will wash away the sins of everyone?"

"O no, only those who come to Him."

"And how can you come to Him, Cathy?"

She was quiet for a minute, and then she said, "I think He will bring me Himself".

Then, about a year after she first became sick, she died; and her soul went straight to heaven. Now she never does anything wrong; she never even thinks anything wrong. God has made her perfect.

Later a friend wrote to her father: "Dear child, she is one of those ransomed ones whose song of praise, I believe, will sound high."

K. D. Macleod

The Rotten Apples

ALLAN's parents taught him the Bible and showed him a good example; so they were worried when they saw him playing with two boys who were sometimes very wicked. His father warned him to keep away from them, but Allan thought that being with them was good fun and would not do him any harm.

One day his father said to him, "Allan, go to the garden and fetch the best apple you can find".

Allan ran to the garden, for he expected to eat the apple. Soon, he returned with a beautiful, rosy apple.

"Put it in that dish," said his father, pointing to an empty bowl. Allan was disappointed but did as he was told.

"Now," said his father, "go and fetch two rotten apples."

Allan thought this a strange request, but he found two rotten apples under the tree and took them to his father.

"Put them with the good apple," said his father.

"O Dad, the rotten apples will spoil the good apple," said Allan, who was still hoping to eat the good apple.

"Just do as I tell you, Allan," said his father.

So Allan obeyed, and his father then took the bowl away.

Some days later Allan and his father looked at the three apples in the bowl. There were the apples, and Allan was sorry to see that the good apple was now rotten and only fit to be thrown away; but that was what he really expected.

"Now Allan," said his father, "this is like what happens to a boy who goes with wicked companions. Just as the good apple became rotten because it was with the rotten ones, so the boy will learn to do wicked things along with his wicked companions.

"The Bible says, 'Evil communications corrupt good manners', or, keeping bad company will spoil good character. The Bible also says, 'The companion of fools shall be destroyed'. So the boy who continues keeping bad company will get worse and worse, and at last he will be cast into hell, just as the rotten apple has to be thrown away. May God give you a new heart so that you would be one of His people and love to be in their company.''

Little
Hidden Things

HAVE you ever seen an ant? Here in Zimbabwe we have many different kinds of ants. The ones which are the biggest nuisance are so tiny you hardly notice them.

In winter it is dry, so the ants are everywhere, searching for food and water. One winter day I poured some soup into a pan only to discover lots of black specks on top. Ants had been in the pan first and I had not noticed them! Yes, they can be a nuisance.

A little while later I felt something on my arm inside my sleeve. Thinking it was another ant I pressed my fingers onto it. Imagine my surprise and dismay when I received a sharp sting. It was a bee!

Sin can be like that. Sometimes we think that sin, like the ant, is no more than a small nuisance, when we get only a scolding for doing what is naughty. But sometimes, we feel that sin is worse. We may feel that it is like the sharp sting of the bee when we suffer punishment or come to harm for our wrongdoing. So we decide to be more careful in future. But is that enough?

Being more careful may prevent bee stings, but sin cannot be dealt with as easily as that! We have done many sins already, and our sins will sting at last in an awful way because our sin will bring us to eternal death. Only Jesus can save us from this deadly sting. He died on the cross of Calvary to save His people from eternal death. It is only those who believe in Him who shall be protected from that deadly sting, for the Bible says that whosoever believes in Him shall not perish, but shall have everlasting life.

I hope that you will seek this safety of everlasting life that only Jesus can give. He says, ''Those that seek me early shall find me'', and, ''Whoso findeth Me findeth life''.

M. Graham

Children Called
to Christ

LIKE mist on the mountain, like ships on the sea,
So swiftly the years of our pilgrimage flee;
In the grave of our fathers how soon we shall lie!
Dear children, today to a Saviour fly.

How sweet are the flowerets in April and May!
But often the frost makes them wither away.
Like flowers you may fade: are you ready to die?
While ''yet there is room'', to a Saviour fly.

When Samuel was young, he first knew the Lord,
He slept in His smile and rejoiced in His Word:
So most of God's children are early brought nigh:
O, seek Him in youth — to a Saviour fly.

Do you ask me for pleasure? Then lean on His breast,
For there the sin-laden and weary find rest.
In the valley of death you will triumphing cry,
''If this be called dying, 'tis pleasant to die!''.

R. M. M'Cheyne

The Coyote Pup

JACK was a hard worker on his father's sheep ranch in Montana. There was always work to be done after school and on Saturdays: sheep to watch, shearing, fences to repair, and other jobs.

One day his father reported that during the last month four lambs were missing. They decided that coyotes must have got them. (Coyotes are small wolves which live in North America.) The number of coyotes had been increasing for the last few years, and now they were causing problems. Although they probably could not kill a full-grown sheep, lambs were an easy catch for a pack of coyotes.

A two-day coyote hunt was organised by Jack's father. Several were found and shot. One of the ranchers found a coyote pup which they also wanted to kill. As Jack watched the pup, it reminded him of a small dog, so cute and helpless. The pup looked at Jack as if it expected him to take care of it. Jack decided that it would make a nice pet for his little sister, Cheryl. He finally got his father to agree to let him keep it, but his father did not like the idea at all. When he finally agreed he reminded Jack, ''It may be a cute puppy now, but it is a coyote, and a coyote it will always be!''.

Jack wrapped the pup in his jacket and carried it back to the ranch for Cheryl. Soon the pup was another member of the ranch and was named Bucky. Everybody, including Jack's father, enjoyed the playful pup. At night Bucky slept near the door since his watchful eyes and good hearing made him a good watchdog. No one really thought of him as a coyote.

One night when Bucky was about a year old, there was a full moon and the night air was cold. Some restless feeling within Bucky stirred him. He went to the edge of the yard and gave the long, mournful cry of the coyote. Jack, who had not gone to sleep yet, heard the call and looked out the window. In the moonlight he could see the shadows of several other coyotes, and without looking back Bucky ran off to them.  Bucky's coyote nature had stirred within him and he had gone to live with his own kind.

Bucky had acted like a dog and lived like a dog. He even looked very much like a dog. But he was a coyote, and he had a coyote's nature.

Some of you may act like a Christian and in every way pass as a Christian, but if you do not know the Lord Jesus Christ as your Saviour, you are not a Christian at all. You were born a sinner, and you have a nature that sins. You may even have Christian parents and live in a home where the Bible is read and obeyed. You may go to Sabbath school and repeat your Bible verses perfectly every week. But, remember, you will always be a guilty sinner in God's sight unless you are born again and believe in the Lord Jesus Christ.

I hope that you are asking God to give you a new nature so that you will be a new creature in Christ Jesus.

Jesus' Arrival in Jerusalem

THERE was a lot of excitement when Jesus raised Lazarus from the dead, and many people came from Jerusalem to see Lazarus. Shortly afterwards, Jesus went up to Jerusalem and the crowds followed Him. On the way He decided to ride on a young ass — but He did not have one. So He sent two of His disciples into a nearby village to borrow one, telling them to say to the owners that He needed it. When the owners heard that, they let the disciples take it. The crowd went on its way and started to cry out about Jesus, from Psalm 118, verses

25 and 26, that He was the King of the Jews. Some of the bad Jews told Jesus to tell them to stop this, but He would not do so.

As they came round the brow of the hill, suddenly Jerusalem burst into view on the other side of the valley. What a beautiful sight! The people were very happy, and more crowds of people were coming out of Jerusalem to meet Jesus. What do you think happened next? Jesus began to cry! What a strange thing to do when everyone else was happy! Why did He cry? Can you think of the reason? It was because He knew that in a few days' time the bad people of Jerusalem would not want Him to be King of the Jews and they would kill Him.

If someone was going to do something bad to you, how would you feel? You would feel sad, and maybe frightened, would you not? But Jesus was not weeping for Himself, but for the bad people. That seems strange to you, does it not? Jesus was weeping for them because He had come to be their King, but they did not want Him to be their King. He would be able to help them, to save them from their sins, but they did not want that help. He was weeping for them, not for Himself.

The crowd of people moved across the valley and into Jerusalem, causing such a stir that people began asking who this was. ''This is Jesus,'' they were told. Then the crowd got bigger and the children also joined it. Where do you think Jesus took the crowds? He went to the Temple, where He saw bad people doing things they should not have been doing there. So Jesus put them out of the Temple, because the Temple was a place for prayer. As he was doing this, the crowd possibly fell silent, wondering what was coming next; but the children continued crying out what they had been learning from the older people, that Jesus was the King of the Jews. *"Hosanna to the Son of David,"* they cried. You can imagine how angry Jesus' enemies were, when they heard this in God's own house, so they told Jesus about it. However, Jesus was quite pleased with the children and He told the Jews that God could bring perfect praise out of the mouths of children.

Now what do you think you can learn from this Bible story?

Firstly, you can learn to *be generous to those that need your help.* Do you remember the owners of the ass? They were generous to lend Jesus their ass.

Secondly, you should *always be ready to give to Jesus when He asks you for something.* Jesus asks you to pray to Him when you begin the day so that He would be with you and help you. You should be willing to give these few moments of your time to Him, although you might wish to spend your time in other ways. When He says to you, "Give Me thine heart", He is asking for your love and obedience.

Thirdly, do you remember Jesus weeping over Jerusalem? Well, you are told to believe in Jesus, to love Him, to follow Him and serve Him. However, if you say that you do not want to do these things, then Jesus cannot be pleased with you, and those who do not have Him as their King and Saviour will be destroyed by their sins and perish in them forever.

Finally, you can see that *Jesus takes notice of the smallest children and He is pleased when they sing the Psalms about Him.* Others might think that, because these small children do not understand, they may as well not sing — but not Jesus!

D. M. Boyd

A Sabbath-breaker
Silenced

PEOPLE break the Sabbath Day when they do things they should not do on that holy day — such things as shopping, playing games and sports, and doing work, like gardening, which does not need to be done on the Lord's Day.

One Sabbath Day, long ago, a godly man in Norfolk saw a man doing work that did not need to be done on a Sabbath. He decided to speak to the Sabbath-breaker to show him how wrong it was to break the Sabbath.

He said to the Sabbath-breaker, ''Suppose I had been working hard all week and earned seven pounds.

Suppose now that I met a poor man and gave him six pounds out of my seven; what would you say to that?''

''I should say that you were very kind,'' he replied, ''and that the man ought to be very thankful.''

''Suppose now,'' said the good man, ''that he was to knock me down and rob me of the other pound. What then?''

The Sabbath-breaker at once said that the thief would deserve to be severely punished.

''Well now,'' said the good man, ''you are just like that thief. God has freely given you six days of the week to work in, and He has kept the seventh day for Himself, so that it would be kept holy by everyone. But you are not satisfied with the six days God has given, and you rob Him of the seventh. What then do you deserve?''

The Sabbath-breaker was silent. He could not make any excuse for working on the Sabbath, because he knew it was wrong and he knew also that he deserved to be punished by God.

When we break the Sabbath Day we should be sorry to God and ask Him to forgive us, for Jesus' sake. I hope that you will love the Sabbath Day and that you will never forget that God tells us, ''Remember the Sabbath Day, to keep it holy''.

God Is
in Heaven

GOD is in heaven. Can he hear
A little prayer like mine?
Yes, that He can; I need not fear;
He'll listen unto mine.

God is in heaven. Can He see
When I am doing wrong?
Yes, that He can; He looks at me
All day and all night long.

God is in heaven. Would He know
If I should tell a lie?
Yes; though I said it very low,
He'd hear it in the sky.

God is in heaven. Does He care,
Or is He good to me?
Yes; all I have to eat and wear
'Tis God that gives it me.

God is in heaven. May I pray
To go there when I die?
Yes, all who seek Him shall one day
Dwell with Him in the sky.

Lessons
from the Birds

ONE very frosty morning there were some birds chirping noisily outside our window. It seemed as if they were asking for more of the good crumbs they had the day before. Someone went out and put crumbs on the bird table, and a crowd of small birds soon gathered. There were lots of chaffinches, a few sparrows, one blackbird, two thrushes, two starlings, and a robin.

Are you, like the birds, asking for good things? You must ask God, ''Give us this day our daily bread''. But are you hungry in your soul? Do you long for such good things as having your soul saved and your sins forgiven? Do you wish to have Jesus as your Saviour? Well, you must ask so that you will receive, and you must seek so that you will find.

I saw that most of the birds busily began their breakfast, but I was surprised at the chaffinches. They were very jealous and greedy and tried to keep all the food for themselves by attacking other birds. They were so busy doing this that they did not have time to enjoy the tasty crumbs.

Are there not some people like the chaffinches? They get plenty good things from God, but they are jealous of other people who get good things. Because of their jealousy they cannot enjoy God's gifts and they also forget to give God thanks for His kindness. We must not be like these chaffinches. We must guard against jealousy and greed, and we must always remember to give thanks to God.

I noticed that the little birds were watching out for danger. Suddenly they would all fly away together with a great flurry. Why? Because a seagull or crow came to help itself from the table. The little birds were afraid to stay on the table in case the big bird attacked them.

We should learn from the little birds to be always on our guard against danger. We must keep away from what is harmful to our bodies, but especially from what is harmful to our souls. There is nothing so dangerous as sin. You must keep away from friends who want you to swear, steal and break the Sabbath. You must avoid reading nasty books and guard against looking at horrible pictures. Most of all, you must find shelter for your soul so that you will be safe from God's punishment for your sins.

When the little birds flew away from danger some of them sheltered under a rhododendron bush. Others went into the dense branches of some shrubs. How clever! They knew that big birds could not get into these places to attack them.

Now, where will you find shelter for your soul? I hope your answer is, ''Only in Jesus''. Always pray to God to make you able to hurry to Jesus and to hide in Him for safety.

What is it to hide in Jesus? It is just to believe in Him. Ask God to make you willing to do this, because no one who believes in Jesus will ever perish.

Of course, you will meet with danger after you believe in Jesus. One day, at nesting time, I heard the frightened cries of some birds. I went out and saw two blackbirds chattering in alarm at something. The cause of their alarm was their enemy, Ginger the cat. I soon chased him away. It was the distress call of the birds which brought someone to help them.

Those of you who are believers must do the same kind of thing when Satan, your enemy, attacks you and when there are other dangers. You must call to God. Indeed, all of you must do this.

Pray to God for help and safety. Be like the man we read about in Psalm 34: ''This poor man cried, God heard, and saved him from all his distresses.'' Pray this prayer from Psalm 16: ''Lord keep me; for I trust in Thee.''

N. M. Ross

Too Late

THIS story is about a Dutch boy called Jacob who was eight years old. He was a nice boy and he was the best pupil in his class. He had lots of friends because he was clever at thinking up different games to play. He was also clever at making things. He used to spend hours working in the shed at home making toys from old pieces of wood.

But Jacob had a bad habit. Whenever anyone called him he would say, "I'm just coming in a minute". When his mother called, "Jacob, go quickly to the shop for me", Jacob would say, "Just coming in a minute, Mum!". Did Jacob come? He did not! If his father called, "Jacob, pump up the tyre of my bike", Jacob said, "Yes, Dad, just in a minute". Did he do it? Not him! Very often he forgot and carried on with what he was doing.

When Jacob had his ninth birthday he got a beautiful present from his parents. It was a tool box filled with all sorts of new, shiny tools. There was a small hammer, a screwdriver, a saw, nails — everything! Jacob was really excited.

Next day was Saturday, so off he went with his new toolbox to the shed. He wanted to make a little garage for his toy cars. He was busy sawing a piece of wood when his mother called, "Jacob, come quickly".

"Just coming in a minute!" Jacob shouted. Everything was just going fine. "Mum will call me again," thought Jacob. "If she doesn't, I will find out later what she wants."

His mother did not call him again; so after a while Jacob thought, "Perhaps I should find out what Mum wants".

He ran into the house.

"You have come at last, Jacob," said his mother. "Grandpa came in the car a little while ago, and he was going to take you to stay with himself and Grandma for the weekend; but when I called, you did not come. Grandpa could not wait; so John has gone with him instead."

Jacob did not answer but turned and went outside. In his eyes were big tears. Had he gone inside when he was called, he would now be with Grandpa in the car. Now it was too late. John had gone instead.

Jacob now made up his mind never to say again, "Just a minute". It was a good lesson he learned that day.

Do you say sometimes, "Just wait a minute"? Take care you do not come too late, just like Jacob. It is bad to wait when you should come right away, or when you should do something at once.

God says, "Remember now thy Creator in the days of thy youth". What do you do? Maybe you think, "I will just wait a while; I will do it some other time". That is a very wrong thing to do because God says, "Remember thy Creator *now*".

In the Bible you are called to seek the Lord early: "Seek ye the Lord, while he may be found." What is your reply? Some boys and girls say, "Not just now. Maybe when I am a little older." That is a dangerous reply because you may not live to be a little older.

The Lord says to young people, "Give me thine heart". What do you say? Perhaps you say, "Some other time — perhaps next week, or next year". But do you not know that it may be forever too late then?

The Frightened Hare

LONG ago in Culloden, near Inverness, there lived a boy whose name we don't know but whose initials were J. M. We shall call him John MacKenzie. When John grew up he told this story about his grandfather, who also lived in Culloden.

One warm day some men were hunting hares with their hounds on Culloden Moor. Two of these dogs spotted a hare and were furiously chasing it. The hare was trying hard to escape by running this way and that.

Suddenly it came to a cottage. It leaped through the open window of the cottage and took refuge under the bed that was in the room.

John's grandfather lived in the cottage. He saw the hare take refuge and he shut the window and door to protect it.

The hunters came to the cottage and demanded that the hare be sent out for the hounds to chase.

"No! no!" said the old man. "The poor hare has sought shelter in my home, and shelter it shall have."

The men had to go away and the hare was safe.

Years later, when John MacKenzie was speaking about what his grandfather did, he said, "O, if there is a

little tenderness like that in a *man's* heart, how great is the tenderness that dwells in the heart of *Jesus!*".

How right he was! There is more tenderness in the heart of Jesus than anyone can tell. We are poor sinners who deserve to be punished forever for our sins. But if we run to Jesus to trust in Him to be our refuge, He will not put us away but will keep us safe. The Bible says, "The name of the Lord (which means Jesus) is a strong tower; the righteous runneth into it and is safe".

Pray that you would be made willing and able to hurry to Jesus to be sheltered from punishment for your sins, and to be safe from the power of Satan. Jesus says, "All that the Father giveth me shall come to Me, and him that cometh to Me I will in no wise cast out".

N. M. Ross

Jesus the Saviour

AND was the Saviour once a child,
A little child like me?
And was He humble, meek and mild,
As little ones should be?

O why did not the Son of God
Come as an angel bright?
And why not leave His fair abode,
To come with power and might?

Because He came not then to reign
As sovereign here below;
He came to save man's soul from sin,
Whence all his sorrows flow.

And did the Son of God most high,
Consent a Man to be?
And did that blessed Saviour die
For sinners such as we?

And did the Saviour freely give
His life for sinful men?
Yes, Jesus died that souls might live;
O, how He loved them then!

New Clothes

I AM sure that when you go back to school after your summer holidays you see many boys and girls with new clothes. In the Bible, clothes are called ''robes'', ''garments'', ''apparel'' and ''raiment''. People in the Bible usually wore long, flowing clothes. Some of you will remember the coat of many colours which Joseph had, and the fine garment which Achan stole.

The Bible tells us about clothes for the soul as well as for the body. Did you know that God says you must have proper clothing to cover your soul? The Bible says that we need to have on ''the robe of righteousness'', ''the wedding garment'', ''the garments of salvation'', and ''white raiment''.

If you are not saved, you are not right before God. Your sins make you bad and filthy. So you must have the robe of the righteousness of Christ to cover your soul, and to make you right before God. When God makes a sinner able to believe in Jesus Christ, He gives him the robe of Christ's righteousness at the same time.

When someone believes in Jesus Christ, it means that he now loves Jesus and is married to Him. So, you see, the robe of righteousness is also the wedding garment for the soul. You will never get into heaven to sit down at the marriage feast at last if you do not have on the wedding garment.

The Bible also teaches that the wedding garment will make you beautiful in your soul. Sin has made you ugly and filthy, and anything which is not clean and beautiful cannot go into heaven. You need the wedding garment to make you fit to go into heaven. A bride looks beautiful in her wedding dress on her wedding day. So all who believe in Jesus will be altogether beautiful in heaven because they will have on the white raiment of saints.

Christ tells you to go to Himself to get this white raiment to cover the shame of your nakedness. Yes, He is most willing to give you this new clothing for your soul. You need it very much. He tells you, ''Ask, and ye shall receive; seek, and ye shall find''.

N. M. Ross

The Kiwi

THE kiwi is found only in New Zealand. Many people living there have never seen one since it hides in its burrow until late evening or night time. Its name comes from its call, ''kee wee'', as it moves about in the darkness.

This is the smallest of all the birds that cannot fly. (The ostrich is the largest.) Although it is a true bird, it looks something like an animal without a tail and even has cat-like whiskers. It is about the size of a chicken and is covered with pretty, soft, grey and brown feathers. (Some people used to make beautiful robes from these feathers, but this is now forbidden.) It has strong legs and feet and can run quickly through the undergrowth. It moves silently, except for a little hissing noise when hunting, and occasionally giving its piercing cry, "kee wee, kee wee".

Although God did not give the kiwi the ability to fly, He gave it special ability to live on the ground.

"But God giveth it a body as it hath pleased Him . . . All flesh is not the same flesh" (1 Corinthians 15:38-39). Since worms and underground insects are its main food, it has been given an unusually long, rough bill to dig with. It hunts mostly in wet or swampy ground, where the digging is easiest. Every other bird has nostrils at the base of its bill, but the kiwi's nostrils are out on the end of its bill. What do you think is the reason for this? Those who have studied this bird believe it smells the food for which it is searching through these openings in its bill. Its small dark eyes do not see much

in the dark, but its keen sense of smell lets it find all its food, including snails, berries and some plants.

If the kiwi was able to think and talk, it would tell us, ''God did not leave out any necessary thing. He has given me all I need to thrive and prosper.'' And it does prosper. Burrowing under the roots of a tree, it builds a nest lined with leaves and grass. It usually lays just one very large white egg which weighs as much as a quarter of the kiwi itself! The kiwi egg is the largest in comparison to its size of any bird on earth.

After laying her egg the female lets the male hatch it. For over two months he stays on the nest, only eating and drinking on quick trips outside, while waiting for the chick to hatch. The hatched chick is covered with soft, dark fuzz called *down*. After only a few days the chick wanders off to make its own way, and the parents forget all about it.

God watches over these strange birds, just as He does over all His creatures. We too are part of His wonderful creation, but unlike the birds and animals, we are responsible to Him for what we do with our lives. He says to you in His Word, ''Remember now thy Creator in the days of thy youth'' (Ecclesiastes 12:1). Also, ''Trust in the Lord with all thine heart; and lean not unto thine own understanding. In all thy ways acknowledge Him, and He shall direct thy paths'' (Proverbs 3:5-6). Are you doing these things?

Samuel Called
to God's Service

SAMUEL was a young boy, possibly no older than some of you who are reading this page. He did not live in his own house but in God's house, the Temple, with an old man called Eli, who was one of God's priests. Samuel lived there because his mother was so pleased God had given her a little boy that she had brought him to help in God's house. Eli would be pleased to get this help.

One night, Samuel had gone to sleep when he was wakened by a voice calling him. So he ran to Eli, but Eli told him that he had not called him and to go back to bed. But, when he did this, Samuel heard the voice calling him again, ''Samuel''. So, thinking it must be Eli this time, he got out of bed the second time and went to Eli. Possibly Eli thought Samuel was dreaming, for he told him to go back to bed again. What do you think happened this time? Yes — he heard the voice calling him again! You can imagine Samuel at first asking himself if he had really heard the voice, but because he was sure that he had heard it he went to Eli for the third time.

Now Eli was a godly old man, and by this time it began to occur to him what was happening. Can you think what was happening? Well, there was someone else in God's house besides Eli and Samuel. It was God Himself. God was calling Samuel. Now the Bible tells us that Samuel did not know God. Think of that! Samuel was helping in God's house, but he did not know God! So Eli told him to lie down again and, if he should hear the voice again, to say, "Speak, Lord; for thy servant heareth". (A servant is someone who works for someone else. Samuel was Eli's servant, and Eli was teaching him these words because he wanted Samuel to work for God also.)

So Samuel lay down again, and God called him by his name again. Maybe, because Samuel did not know God, he was a little frightened, for he did not repeat exactly what Eli said; but he did say, "Speak; for thy servant heareth", which shows that he was ready to listen to God.

This was the beginning of Samuel listening to God and working for God. There is more about Samuel in the Bible, where we read about his famous life as one of God's servants. You may read about it in the Old Testament, in the First Book of Samuel.

Now, we can also learn a few lessons from this story:

First, you may feel that you are too small for God to pay attention to you. You may feel that He only pays attention to adults, the "grown-ups". But this little story shows that *God pays attention to children and speaks to them.* Now, you know that God speaks to us nowadays in the Bible and this story shows us that *God wants you to listen to the Bible* and, when you are old enough to do so, to read it yourself.

Second, we see that Samuel did not realise that it was God speaking to him, even though he was in God's house. There are many people nowadays who, when they read the Bible, do not realise that it is God who is speaking to them, even though it is God's Book which they read. So you should remember that, *when you read or hear the Bible, God is speaking to you.*

Third, although Samuel lived in God's house, he did not know God. *It may be that you who are reading this page do not know God.* Although you have been told about God, although you go to God's house and you read the Bible, it may be that you do not know God. If this is so, you should follow the advice that Eli gives to Samuel, which is the next lesson.

Fourth, Eli taught Samuel to pray to God. This is what you must do. You must pray to God and be willing to listen to Him and do as He says. God is telling you to believe in Jesus for the forgiveness of your sins and to turn from all your bad ways, and then you will be one of His servants. I hope you enjoy helping God's people, as Samuel enjoyed helping Eli; but *I hope you also want to serve God,* to work for Him. Are you listening to Him and doing as He says? All those who listen to and obey God's Word are His servants. They may do different jobs in this world, but they are all God's servants. Wouldn't you like to be one of them?

D. M. Boyd

Should Henry get a Good Thrashing?

I AM not sure if the boy's name was Henry or not, but that is what we are going to call him. One day he went out to play and spent his time climbing trees. He was trying to reach the nests which the rooks had built in the trees. Probably it was not very safe to do that; Henry might quite easily have fallen and broken his leg or his arm, if he was not very careful. Anyway, a man who lived in one of the next houses saw him up in the trees. He thought that Henry was a very bad boy, so he decided to go and tell his father.

The man arrived at the manse door — Henry's father was a minister called Mr. Bonar. He told Mr. Bonar about what he had seen Henry doing. The man was not pleased himself and he thought Mr. Bonar should be very angry too. He told him, ''I hope you will give the boy a good thrashing''. What do you think Mr. Bonar said to the man? He asked him, ''If I thrashed the boy for that, what would I do if he told me a lie?''.

Now I don't think Mr. Bonar would have liked Henry to do anything that was dangerous, or to go to any place where he might fall and hurt himself badly. But he was sure that telling lies was something far, far worse.

What do you think about telling lies? Do you ever think about it? Do you know what God thinks about it? God tells us in the Bible not to tell lies. He says, "Lie not one to another". God tells us too that He is going to punish liars, that He will even punish those who tell what they think are just very little lies. He says, "A false witness shall not be unpunished, and he that speaketh lies shall not escape".

Mr. Bonar believed what God says about lies, and so should we. If we tell lies, God wants us to stop. And there is something else we must do too — we must tell God about our lies. We must tell Him that we know it is wrong to tell lies, that it is sin. And we must ask Him to forgive us for Christ's sake.

K. D. Macleod

50

Little Things

A LITTLE, 'tis a little word,
But much may in it dwell;
Then let the warning truth be heard:
O learn the lesson well.

The way of ruin thus begins,
Down, down, like easy stairs,
If conscience suffers little sins,
Soon larger ones it bears.

A little theft, a small deceit,
Too often leads to more;
'Tis hard at first, but tempts the feet,
As through an open door.

Just as the broadest rivers run
From small and distant springs,
The greatest crimes that men have done
Have grown from little things.

The child who early disobeys,
Stands now on slippery ground;
And who shall tell, in future days,
How low he may be found?

Number Our Days

EACH Sabbath evening during school term here at Ingwenya in Zimbabwe, we have an English service. Sometimes it is taken by Mr. Mpofu, the technical teacher and boarding master. Recently he spoke to the pupils about verse 12 of Psalm 90, which says, "So teach us to number our days, that we may apply our hearts unto wisdom". It was remarkable, as well as solemn and sad, that one of the pupils died from cancer not long after this talk was given. Here are a few things Mr. Mpofu said to us that Sabbath evening.

"We all make plans for the future and we don't think that our days are numbered. We do not know what the number of our days is, but God knows it. We all have known people whose end has come even although they had lots of plans for the future. Their days were numbered — when God's time came they had to go! . . .

"When you bring your desks for repair to my workshop I see some of you have a timetable for your work stuck inside — so much time to be spent on each subject. You know that if you are to pass your exams you must plan your time. You have to count the time until the exam and prepare for it. What would you think of a boy or girl who thought, 'Exams are a long time away', and who did no work but just played around? They would not be able to cope later on and get their work up-to-date. Exam time would find them unprepared. . . .

"I remember a little story we have for children. An ant and a grasshopper played together in summer when everything was green. The ant also prepared for winter by storing food; but the grasshopper, seeing plenty of leaves to eat, thought this was not necessary. Then winter came and everything dried up. The ant went down a hole into his nest and lived on what he had prepared. When he came out of his nest in spring he saw his friend, the grasshopper, lying dead on the ground. He had made no preparation until it was too late. . . .

"We do not know the number of our days, and so we must pray this prayer, 'Teach us to number our days . . . '. We need the Holy Spirit to teach us that the number of our days is much less than we think, and that we must apply our hearts to wisdom without delay. We must seek and have this true wisdom of knowing Jesus Christ and believing in Him. Then our sins will be forgiven and we will have eternal life; and we will be prepared for the judgment. . . .

"When people who belong to the Lord are making plans they say, 'If the Lord will'. They say this because they know that their times are in the Lord's hands and that He may call them away at any time. . . .

"So we need to learn these important lessons:

(1) Our days are numbered and only God knows the number.

(2) We need to ask Him to teach us to number our days.

(3) When He will teach us to number our days then we will learn wisdom to prepare for when our days come to an end.

(4) Our days may come to an end much sooner than we think.

(5) We need to remember that we will be judged, so we must be ready to meet God when our time is up.

"Let us start now, even in church here, to pray this prayer: 'O Lord, teach us to number our days, that we may apply our hearts unto wisdom.' "

M. Graham

A Slippery Road

THERE must have been heavy rain during the night, then the skies cleared, and the water which could not run off the road very soon froze solid in long thick sheets of ice. So the next morning when I came along in my car, just a few days ago, the road was very dangerous. And when I came back in the evening I felt it was even more dangerous as it was now dark.

I had just turned a corner, and I saw a long icy stretch of road in front of me. I thought that this road was just like my life stretching out before me.

Why did I think that?

Because if I had walked on that icy road I would very likely have slipped and fallen. And how easy it is for us to fall into sin! Especially if we think we will get on well in life by our own efforts. But could I not walk perfectly safely even on that slippery road if someone greater than I am had been supporting me from the side of the road, always ready to steady me if I slipped?

Believers have Someone who does just that for them as they walk through life. In fact, the Bible speaks of believers leaning on their Beloved One, Jesus Christ. It is the only safe way to live our lives.

Here is a verse for you to learn:

Hold up my goings, Lord, me guide
In those Thy paths divine,
So that my footsteps may not slide
Out of those ways of Thine.

(Psalm 17:5)

Make this verse your own prayer. And ask God too that He would make you one of His children, who believe in Him and lean on Him.

K. D. Macleod

Some
Australian Birds

On my first morning in Grafton, Australia, I was wakened about five o'clock by what I thought was people quarrelling outside. It was daylight, and when I looked out I saw that it was not people but birds who were making the noise. They were Noisy Friar Birds — a very suitable name. Their call sometimes sounds like, "It's half past four!". The bird book said, "They squabble and show off like a bunch of naughty school-boys". That is just what they were doing that morning. Don't you think that squabbling and showing off by boys and girls can upset other people? I did not like being wakened at five o'clock by Noisy Friar Birds saying, "It's half past four! It's half past four!". And I'm sure your Mum or Dad does not like it when you are showing off or quarrelsome. Remember that the Bible says, "Be ye kind one to another".

Another bird is the Laughing Kookaburra. Its nickname is "The Laughing Jackass", and its call is like a cackling laugh. This laughing call may be heard at any time of the day. For you and me there is a time to laugh, and there is also a time not to laugh. You laugh when you are having a happy time with good friends, but it is not right to laugh at people because they may not be as clever or strong as you are. Also, we should never laugh at wicked things, and we should never laugh at holy things.

I was walking across a park in Sydney one day when I met the Australian Magpie, and I did not enjoy meeting it! The bird dived to attack me and then flew to a tree. Three times it swooped down, and I had to duck very quickly! Why was it attacking me? The bird book said, "During the breeding season they fiercely defend their territory against other animals, including man". Yes, the magpie thought I was coming to rob its nest in the tree, but I had no thought of doing any harm. I'm afraid some people are like the magpie — they are suspicious for no reason and they are ready to attack others for no cause. We must be careful not to jump to wrong conclusions or wrongly accuse others.

Have you heard of an Australian bird that sounds like a bell? It is a shy bird, so it is often heard before it is seen; and what a beautiful sound it makes! Its call is a pure note like the "ting" of a silver bell. You will not be surprised if I tell you that it is called the Bell Bird. Now, just as a pure sound comes from the throat of the Bell Bird, so good words should come from our mouths. Do you know which words are bad words? Swear words, lying words, quarrelling words and boasting words are all bad words. The Bible says, "Let no corrupt communication proceed out of your mouth, but that which is good". That means you must not let bad words come out of your mouth, and that you must speak good words. Ask God to make you able to speak good words.

N. M. Ross

Vanie's and Annie's
Answered Prayer

LONG ago, in an American town, two sisters, one about five, the other older, went to a shop each Saturday for their mother. One morning they were returning home when Vanie, the elder one, became suddenly ill with very severe cramps. She was in great pain and could not go a step further. There were only factories nearby and everyone was busy inside. Not a person was to be seen, and the girls did not know what to do. Annie was too shy to go into one of the factories for help, so they sat quietly for a while — at least as quietly as the pain would allow.

Suddenly Vanie said, ''Annie, you know that a good while ago Mother told us that if we were ever in trouble we should pray, and God would help us. Now you help me to go on my knees and we will pray.''

There on the street, these two children asked God to send someone to help them home. Then they sat down, waiting for the answer to their prayer.

Soon Annie saw a man come out of a factory far down the street. He looked around and up and down the street, and then went back into the factory.

''O, he has gone in again,'' said Annie.

''Well,'' said Vanie, ''perhaps he is not the one God is going to send. If he is, he will be back again.''

''There he comes again,'' said Annie. ''He comes this way. He seems to be looking for something. He walks slow. O, he has gone in again. What shall we do?''

''That may not be the one whom God will send to help us,'' said Vanie. ''If he is, he will come out again.''

''O, there he is again,'' said Annie. ''He comes this way.''

He looked at them kindly and asked in a broken German accent, ''Children, what is the matter?''.

''O sir,'' said Annie, ''my sister here is so sick she cannot walk and we cannot get home.''

"Where do you live, my dear?"

"Away at the end of this street."

"Never mind," said the man, "I take you home."

So the strong man carried her home. Annie ran to her mother to tell her that there was a man at the door wishing to see her. The astonished mother took charge of the precious bundle, and the child was laid on a bed.

After thanking the man, she expected him to leave; but he still stood there as if he wished to say something. She thanked him again and asked, "Would you like me to pay you for bringing my child home?".

"O, no," he said, "God pays me! God pays me! I would like to tell you something, but my English is so poor I am afraid you will not understand."

The mother assured him that she would understand.

"I own the ink factory on this street," he said. "I was working very hard at my account books, anxious to be ready in time to pay my men. Suddenly I could not see the figures. The writing in the book all ran together, and I had a strong feeling that someone outside in the street wished to see me. I went out, looked around, but I saw no one and went back to my desk. But I could not see the figures again, and the impression was stronger than before that someone in the street needed me. I went out again, walked a little way, puzzled to know what it meant. Unable to solve the mystery, I went back into my office. This time my fingers were unable to hold the pen, and the impression was stronger than ever on my mind that someone needed my help. I went out and walked some distance till I came opposite the children, and I found that there was indeed need of my help."

As the kind man was about to leave the house, the younger girl said, "Mother, we prayed". And so the mystery was solved. The man was deeply moved — even to tears.

I have enjoyed many happy talks with Annie in her house, for she now has her own home. She and Vanie live in the same city, earnest Christian mothers who teach their children the things of God. I hope their children will have like faith in God; and that you also will trust in the Lord, who heard these children when they prayed.

Jeign Arrh (abridged)

Rainy Season
Story

RAIN comes in Zimbabwe only between October and April. The rest of the year we never use a raincoat or an umbrella! This may seem good, but when it is very hot we long for rain.

Some years very little rain falls and there is famine, but this year plenty has fallen and many people should have a good harvest.

However, this is not always true and we can learn a lesson from the different people we see around.

Mr. Hlakanipi has his field ploughed and is ready to plant whenever the first shower comes so that his crops benefit from every drop of rain. He cultivates properly and a good harvest is the result.

Mr. Thandabuza wants to be sure that the rain will come and that it will not stop soon, so he waits too long and then plants. If later rains do not come his crop is lost!

Mr. Ivila makes excuses of previous droughts and does not plant at all, and even when others are eating fresh green mealies (corn on the cob) his family is still hungry.

I ought to tell you that the names of these men have meanings. Hlakanipi means ''wise'', Thandabuza